ookie
out® Math

Patterns
Everywhere

By Julie Dalton

Consultant
Ari Ginsburg
Math Curriculum Specialist

Children's Press®
A Division of Scholastic Inc.
New York   Toronto   London   Auckland   Sydney
Mexico City   New Delhi   Hong Kong
Danbury, Connecticut

Designer: Herman Adler Design
Photo Researcher: Caroline Anderson
The photo on the cover shows a girl holding a kebab made of fruit lined up
in a pattern.

Library of Congress Cataloging-in-Publication Data

Dalton, Julie, 1951–
    Patterns everywhere / by Julie Dalton ; consultant, Ari Ginsburg.
        p. cm. — (Rookie read-about math)
    Includes index.
    ISBN 0-516-25266-6 (lib. bdg.)   0-516-25367-0 (pbk.)
    1. Sequences (Mathematics)—Juvenile literature. 2. Pattern perception—
Juvenile literature. I. Ginsburg, Ari. II. Title. III. Series.
    QA292.D35 2005
    515'.24—dc22   2005004626

Grandma is making a quilt. Ella is watching.

Grandma cuts fabric into squares. She makes three piles.

In the first pile, she puts blue squares. In the second pile, she puts yellow squares. In the last pile, she puts green squares.

6

Grandma sews a blue
square and a yellow
square together.

Then she adds a green square. Then she adds a blue one. Then she adds a yellow one.

Blue, yellow, and green. Blue, yellow, and . . . what color will be next?

Green!

Grandma adds a green square.

Grandma tells Ella that this is the pattern of the quilt.

Ella goes outside. She thinks about patterns.

She looks at the stone path. One stone, two stones, one stone, two stones . . .

13

The stone path has a pattern! 1, 2, 1, 2 . . .

Ella wants to find more patterns.

Ella looks at the wallpaper
in her room.

Ella has found another
pattern!

18

Ella wants to make a pattern herself.

She strings one red bead. Next to the red bead, Ella puts two green beads.

Next to the two green beads, Ella places three yellow beads.

Ella does the pattern again. One red bead, then two green beads.

What is next?

One red bead, two green beads, three yellow beads, one red bead, two green beads . . .

Three yellow beads are next!

Ella has made a pattern!

Ella gets a marker
and paper.

She writes the numbers
of the pattern.

It has been a busy day
for Ella.

She has learned that
patterns are everywhere.

They are even where
she sleeps.

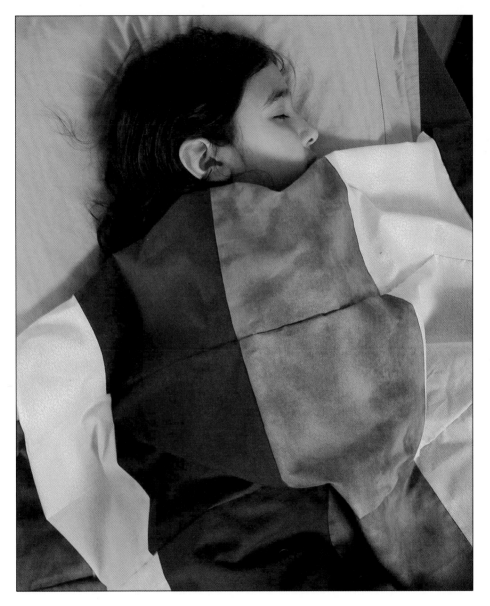

Words You Know

beads

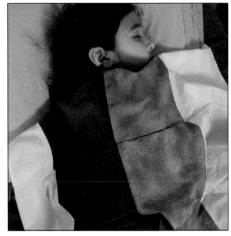

fabric

pattern

quilt

squares

stone path

wallpaper

Index

About the Author

Julie Dalton is an editor and writer who lives in central Connecticut. She lives with her big, hairy dog, a gentle cat, and several teenagers.

Photo Credits

All photographs © 2005 Jay Mallin Photos